PETER RANDALL-PAGE

AT YORKSHIRE SCULPTURE PARK

27 JUNE 2009 – JANUARY 2010
UNDERGROUND GALLERY & LAWN / GARDEN GALLERY

For Joan Randall-Page

Exhibition guide
supported by:

THE ROGER
DE HAAN
CHARITABLE TRUST

YSP

Introduction

Clare Lilley, Head Curator

This is an extensive project by one of Britain's most distinctive and singular sculptors. Peter Randall-Page's connection with Yorkshire Sculpture Park began in 1984 when he was included in the group exhibition, Attitudes '84. Eight years later an iconic selection of his sculpture was shown on the Formal Terrace, as a sister project to the large survey exhibition organised by the Henry Moore Centre for the Study of Sculpture at Leeds City Art Gallery. Since then we have shown individual works and Peter has realised many important projects, including major works for the public realm, such as the Millennium Seed Bank, the Eden Project, and the University of Cardiff. The current exhibition has been some years in the making, with the opening of Yorkshire Sculpture Park's Underground Gallery in 2005 as the catalyst for envisaging this particular selection. For an artist whose work is more commonly seen outdoors, both in public and private spaces, the galleries represent to Peter an opportunity and challenge to show existing pieces in a new context, and to create new, large scale work. Most especially, Peter has used the exhibition as an opportunity to realise a series of extraordinary wall works in clay, thereby extending his practice.

This is not a survey and the majority of sculptures in the gallery and on the lawns around it are recent or new, whilst reflecting on and given context by some earlier drawings and sculptures. A rhythm runs through the spaces, from the spare presentation of the massive Kilkenny limestones in the first gallery, through the obdurate grittiness of flint, granite and fired clay pieces in the largest, central space, and on to the respective dramatic colour and sublime subtlety of painted and bronze works in the last gallery. In the ancillary Project Space is evidence of the fantastic physical and thought processes within Peter's work, as well as a body of new small clay sculptures that he has developed from thrown pots.

The Garden Gallery comprises sculptures and works on paper from Peter's archive and these, too, give context to the broader exhibition. The rectilinear lawns around the gallery are effectively outdoor gallery spaces. Here, new and recent sculptures stand against the tall and dense yew hedge which borders the space, where they are animated by the Yorkshire light and weather.

The concerns that have prevailed for over thirty years in Peter's work are played out here with the greatest richness and strength. For millennia humans have sought to impose order on the apparent chaos of our world. Whilst chaotic motion does exist in both nature and in mathematics, modern science also shows the extraordinary inherent order within the natural world and it is with this geometry, sequencing and rhythm that Peter is absorbed and which manifests itself within his work. However, while always informed by these patterns and forms, his work goes far beyond the botanical or animalistic. He delves into the mathematics that is woven into the fabric of the natural world and in so doing explores symmetry, camouflage, tessellations; the unity and dissonance of the positive and negative; he examines time and chthonic forces; the abundance, sexuality and sensuality of nature are brought to bear; music in its variations threads through the sculpture and drawings. All these and more come together in this mature body of highly provocative and contemplative works.

We are most grateful to the lenders to the exhibition: Tate; Roger and Lyvie De Haan; the Saïd Business School, Oxford; Southend-on-Sea Borough Council; Julian Francis; Warwick Arts Centre, and private collectors. Elsewhere in this guide, the artist acknowledges the support of many others, including his own and YSP staff to whom I also extend my gratitude. For their financial contribution to the exhibition and its supporting publications, I am most grateful to: Arts Council England, Yorkshire; the Henry Moore Foundation; Romulus Construction Ltd; Friends of Yorkshire Sculpture Park; Simon and Virginia Robertson; The Roger De Haan Charitable Trust; Julian Francis; Gay McGuinness; Edward Miller and Monina von Opel. This exhibition represents enormous effort, planning and stamina on the part of the artist and those who work with him. It has been an immense privilege and pleasure to work with Peter Randall-Page and to him I offer our greatest thanks.

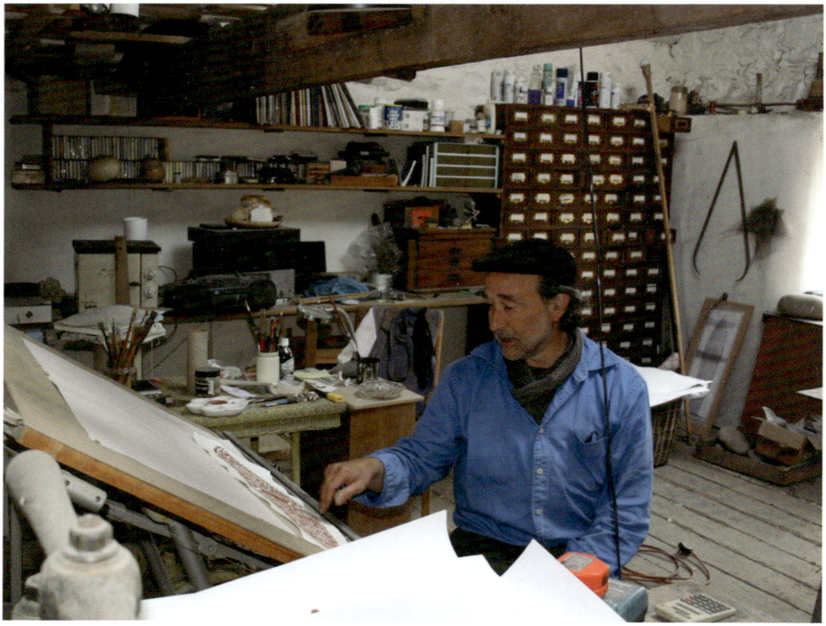

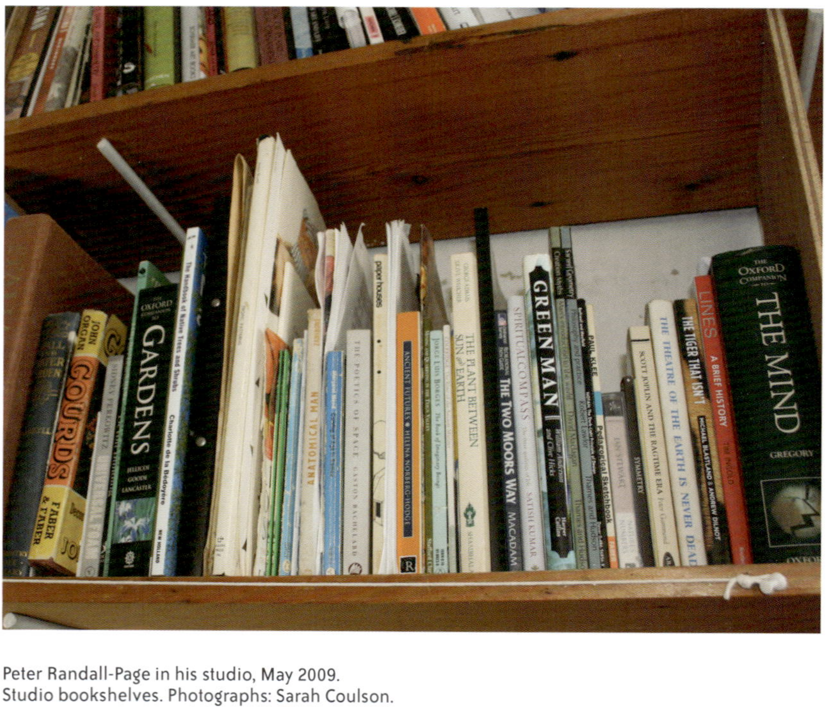

Peter Randall-Page in his studio, May 2009.
Studio bookshelves. Photographs: Sarah Coulson.

Peter Randall-Page at Yorkshire Sculpture Park

Sarah Coulson, Assistant Curator

Peter Randall-Page is a perceptive, intelligent artist who takes the detailed study of the themes with which he is concerned particularly seriously; his bookshelves abound with titles on plants, geometry, mathematics, fossils, philosophy, art, music, history, patterns. He has an enquiring mind and a relentless desire to understand the minutiae of the world around him. His most passionate preoccupation is with the natural world; the close study of organic form is at the centre of his artistic practice. In recent years his interest in naturally occurring pattern and the dynamic tension between order and chaos has led to a series of works that focus on pattern as something fundamental to the emergence of life and growth.

All these ideas, and a lifetime of accruing knowledge across multifarious disciplines, feed into everything that Peter Randall-Page makes; yet, despite the incredible complexity of thought behind them, the works are immediately accessible on an intuitive, instinctual level. Even if we do not understand the mathematics or the geometry, we relate to them subjectively on an utterly different level of comprehension. Randall-Page states, "plants, in common with the rest of the world, enter our consciousness as subjective feelings as well as more quantifiable information; we recognise them as an aspect of the biological system of which we ourselves are part; they nourish our spirits as well as our bodies and stimulate our imaginations as well as our intellects".[1] As an artist, Randall-Page wants more than anything else to convey metaphor without recourse to words and to appeal directly to the unifying elements of existence that make us all human. He says, "I want my forms to function as a psychological investigation, which hopefully will strike a chord of recognition in the viewer. I'm an absolute rationalist. I don't believe in a collective unconscious in the strictly Jungian sense, but it would be pretty remarkable if certain forms didn't have a resonance since we share an evolutionary history". [2]

1 'In the Realm of the Senses: Paul Nesbitt in conversation with Peter Randall-Page', June 1996. From Peter Randall-Page In Mind of Botany, 1996. pg 3.
2 Peter Randall-Page in an interview with Brian McAvera in Sculpture, July/August 2003 vol. 22, no. 6.

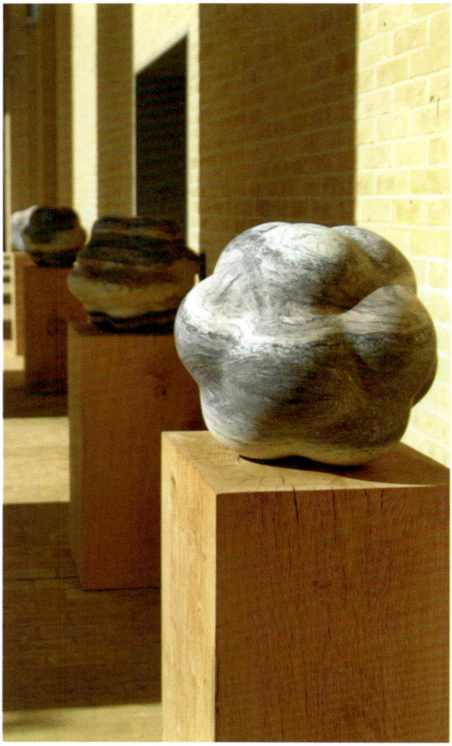

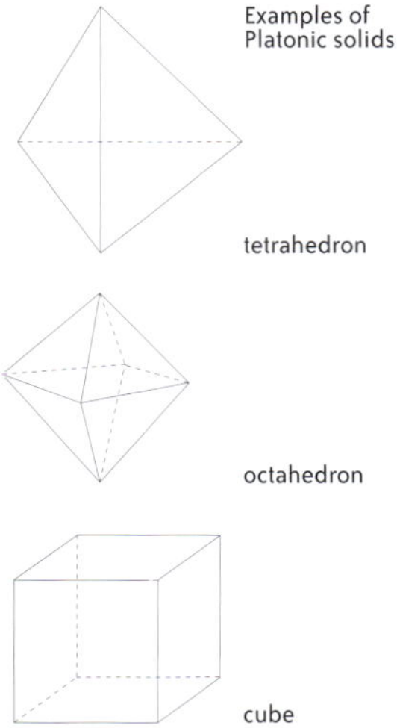

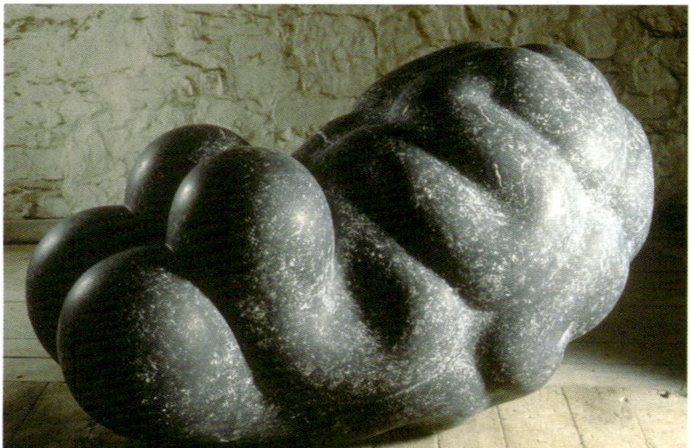

Shapes in the Clouds (Plato Dreaming of Artemis), 2005.
Loan: the Collection of the Saïd Business School. Photograph: Greg Smolonski.
Where the Bees Sucks, 1991. Loan: Tate: preserved by the Trustees of the Chantrey Bequest, 1993.
Photograph: Chris Chapman.

Underground Gallery

Shapes in the Clouds (Plato Dreaming of Artemis), 2005, is made of extraordinary Rosso Luana marble from near Carrara, Italy. Heavily figured, with captivating coloured veining, looking at this work might feel like looking into the universe in miniature, or into a solid cluster of sky. The formal shapes of the sculptures, based on four of the five Platonic solids and sharing the same geometry, contain this seemingly endless material, introducing structure and regularity to the boundless vitality of the stone. Yet the works remain manifestly sensual, a fact that is reflected in the subtitle. Artemis was the Greek goddess of fertility and childbirth, and in early representations was depicted as a many-breasted figure. Randall-Page's voluptuous sculptural forms clearly resonate with this idea.

Where the bee sucks, there suck I:
In a cowslip's bell I lie;
There I couch when owls do cry.
On the bat's back I do fly
After summer merrily.
Merrily, merrily shall I live now
Under the blossom that hangs on the bough.

Where the Bees Sucks, 1991, comes from a song sung by Ariel, a sprite in Shakespeare's The Tempest who is anticipating returning to the natural world after being a servant. The song revels in bounteous, fecund nature, and Randall-Page's sculpture also conveys a sense of ripeness and fertility. Yet it is almost too ripe and the coiled form behind the sensuously alluring bulbous flower-like shape appears simultaneously serpentine and reminiscent of the abdomen of an insect. The temptation of Eve comes to mind and there is a menace about the work.

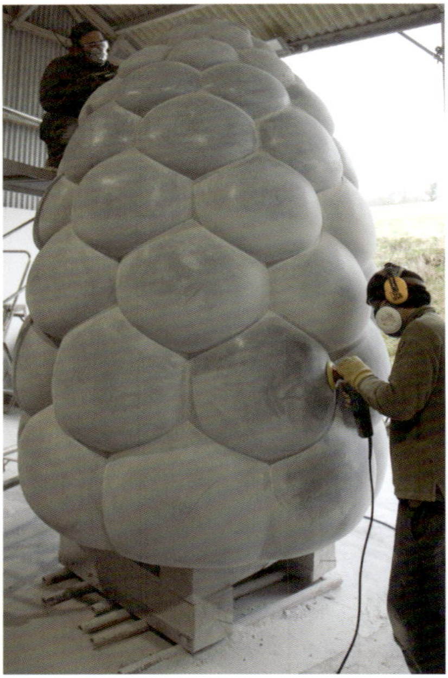

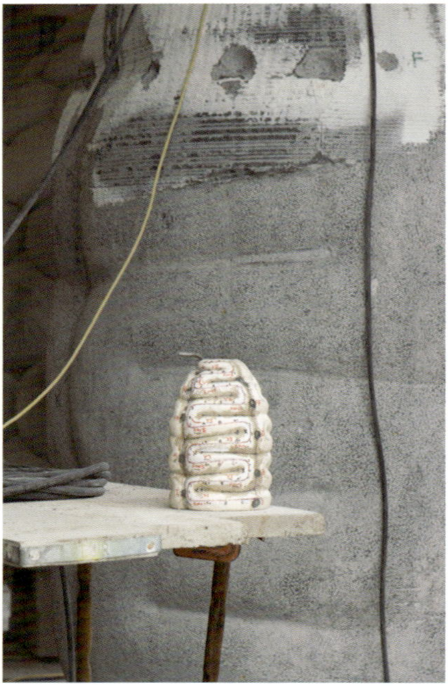

Fructus, 2009. Corpus, 2009.
Photographs: Chris Chapman.

Underground Gallery

Fructus and Corpus, 2009

Kilkenny limestone was first used by Peter Randall-Page in the mid-1980s. Its remarkable surface quality make it ideal when alluding to the possibility of animate life being contained within the stone, its taut surface appearing to bulge and strain at a containing membrane, like an embryo in a yolk sack. A dark, fine textured, grey-blue sedimentary rock, it is flecked with tiny white fossils whose presence is evidence of its several million year history.

These two powerful new sculptures embody distinct, recurring ideas within Peter Randall-Page's work: the endless and coiling line, symmetry, and imagined forms which fall between abstraction and approximating organic shapes. Corpus obviously relates to the body and has a visceral energy that is compressed and compacted like a coiled spring within a taut skin. Its forms are elemental – they hint at many things but resist being the literal embodiment of any of them; snakes, worms, intestines, or the brain. As the voluptuous, fleshy line doubles in on itself it creates points of touch – always imbued with a particular charge – and in Corpus they vitalise the work. Just as the body and the brain are symmetrical, Corpus is divided into two lobes, mirrored at either side of a central line and seeming to grow from it.

Fructus appears as a throbbing mass: a fruit or seed or a cluster of dividing cells, it literally bulges with the potential for life. Like a ripe fruit it is also on the cusp of tipping over the threshold to become overripe or rotten. Randall-Page skillfully explores the relationship between surface and volume, implying both life and substance in this inanimate material.

Underground Gallery
Gallery Two

Glacial granite boulder works, 2007-2009

The central gallery space constitutes a marked change in tempo and texture, with the igneous granite and brick clay works differing dramatically from the cool, smooth sedimentary Kilkenny in the first gallery. Rugged, almost brutal, and cut with often harsh geometric lines or shapes, the granite is coarse grained with a rough, open structure. For Randall-Page each stone is a foil for a very different kind of idea: these found glacial boulders are pivotal to the expression of his interest in the precarious balance between order and chaos found in the natural world. The form of these stones is mathematically random, having been shaped within glaciers and by their environment for millennia, but the carving is ordered and regular. These lines represent all manner of naturally occurring patterns, from the hexagons of cypress cones to chemical reactions.

Sourced mostly from Finland, the boulders retain the memory of their history. Randall-Page does not alter the original contours of the stone; instead he cuts into the surface, drawing attention to the form by the application of lines or simple shapes. The pairing of Inhalation and Exhalation with their respective concave and convex cylinders implies movement in the stone, akin to primordial breathing.

Set in clusters, the works build a visual relationship, with different textures, colours and densities of carving. Each new stone relates to the next and the effect swells across the gallery space.

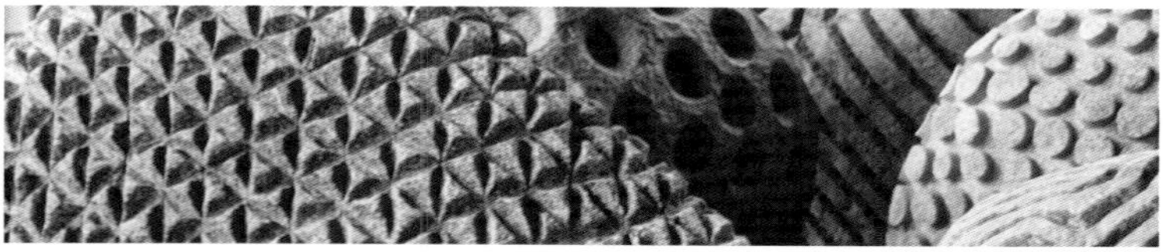

Sculpture in the studio, 2008. Photograph: Peter Randall-Page.

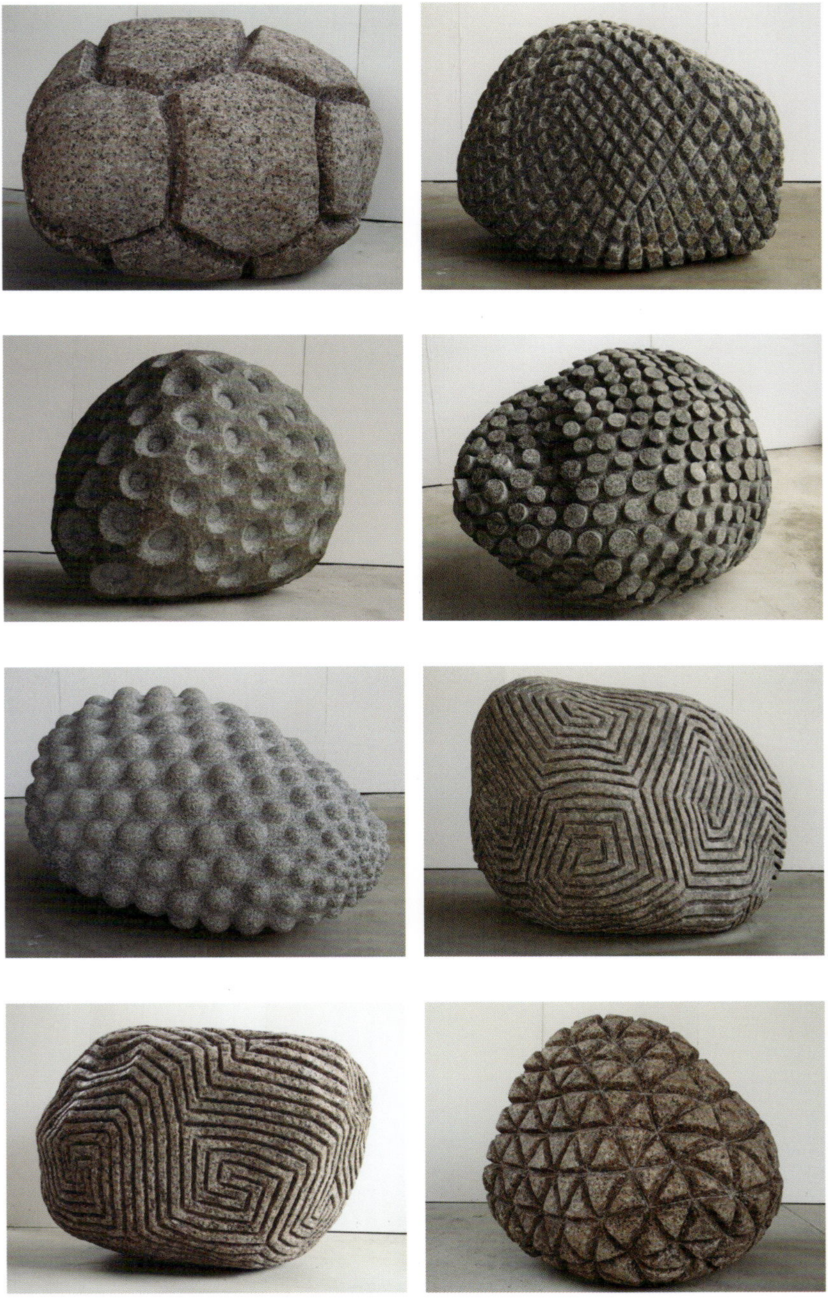

Left to right, from top: Cupressus I, 2008. Pythagoras Stone, 2007. Inhalation, 2008. Exhalation, 2008. Little Seed, 2007. Skin Deep I, 2007. Skin Deep II, 2008. Triangulation II, 2008. Photographs: Ben Adams.

Anatomies of Thought, 1994

Originally made for Prittlewell High School in Essex, Anatomies of Thought is one of only a few architectural reliefs by Randall-Page and was rescued prior to the demolition of the school. A false wall has been built around the work to reflect its original position where it was integral to the façade of a building.

Made of sawn Portland stone inlaid with knapped flints to create a stark contrast in both colour and texture, this imposing work epitomises concerns central to the artist's work in the mid-1990s. During this period the projection of organic forms onto a flat surface was being investigated in split boulder works, as was the creation of cipher-like characters reminiscent of ancient rock art or hieroglyphs, and the idea of cutting open a bud or seed to reveal the densely packed beginnings of life within.

The coiled line without end also recalls the mythical serpent Ouroborus which ate its own tail, its body then forming a continuous loop.

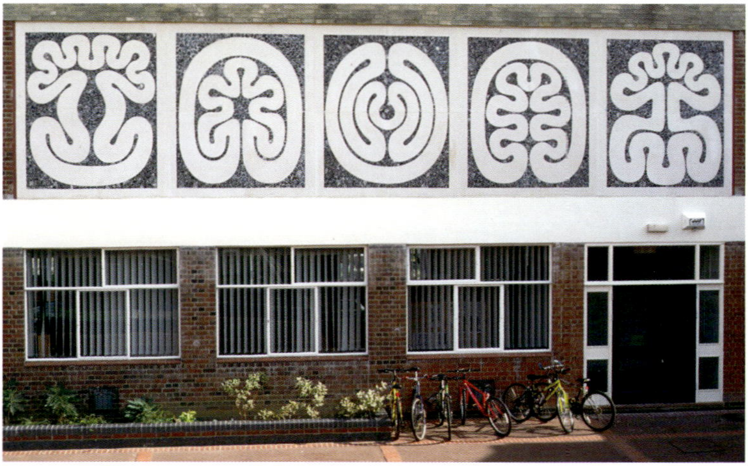

Anatomies of Thought, 1994. Commissioned by Essex County Council for Prittlewell High School. Photograph: Donato Cinicolo 3.

Wing, 2009

Wing is based on a microscopic study of a grasshopper wing, with each small tile in the panel representing an element of the wing's intricate cellular structure. As with other works by Randall-Page the viewer is presented with a magnification of nature's minutiae; the invisible or barely visible building blocks of nature presented on a human scale.

Symmetrical down a central axis, each tile of the wing has been cut according to the artist's drawing and then sliced in two with wire, forming two near-identical pieces that mirror one another in form, texture and colour.

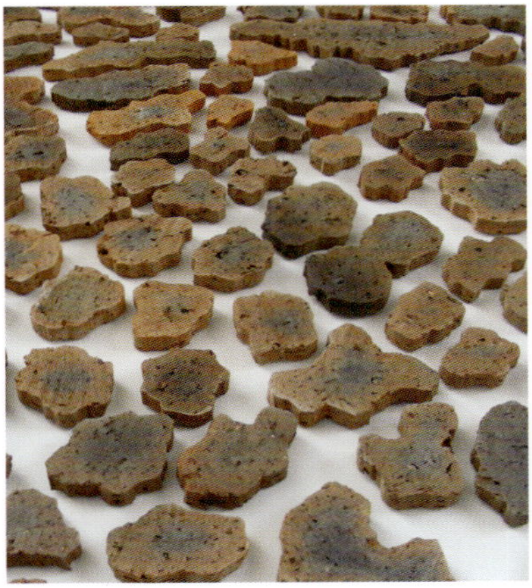

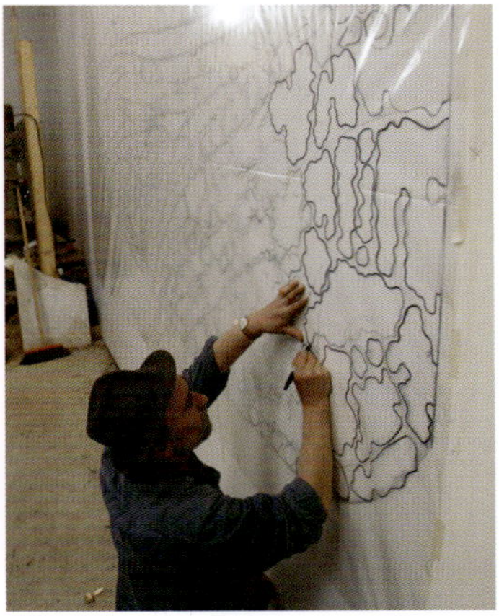

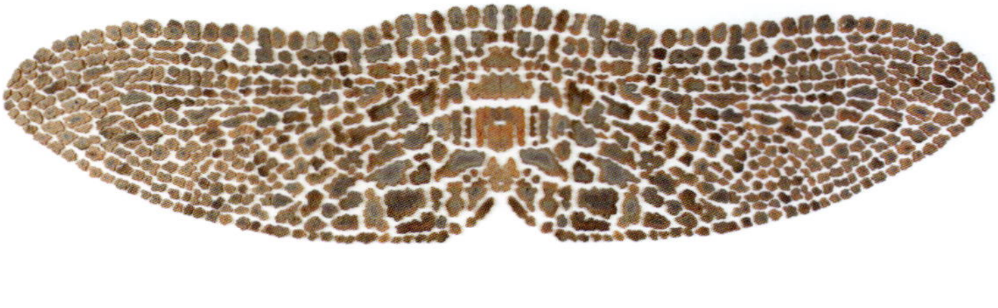

Wing (detail), 2009. Photograph: Adrianne Neil.
Peter Randall-Page working on the drawing for Wing. Photograph: Chris Chapman.
Wing, 2009. Photograph: Jonty Wilde.

Mind Map, 2009

The Mind Map wall works developed out of Randall-Page's Euclidian Egg series of Rorschach ink-blot style drawings in paint. Greek mathematician Euclid (c. 300BC) set out a system for creating compass and straight edge constructions, including egg shapes made up of intersecting lines and circles. The striking patterns formed within the shapes are revealed across the Mind Map series.

Made of fired brick clay, the works have a coarse texture and striking colouring. Even the fabrication of the individual tiles reflects the original symmetrical drawings, with each half of the egg made as an exact mirror image of the other by bisecting every clay slab and then placing the two pieces on either side of the central axis. The patterns and relationships that are established across the surface of Mind Map, as in Mind's Eye, make us aware of the cognitive processes occurring in our brains as we assimilate the complexities of what we see before us. Randall-Page says, "pattern can reveal something universal about the way the human imagination works. In fact, one could say that pattern recognition is fundamental to human consciousness: it underpins mathematics, language, and our perception of time and space." [3]

The captivating, intricate shapes also call to mind many other associations, particularly cross-sections of the brain or the heart as seen through advanced scanning equipment.

3 Peter Randall-Page in an interview with Brian McAvera in Sculpture, July/August 2003 vol.22, no. 6.

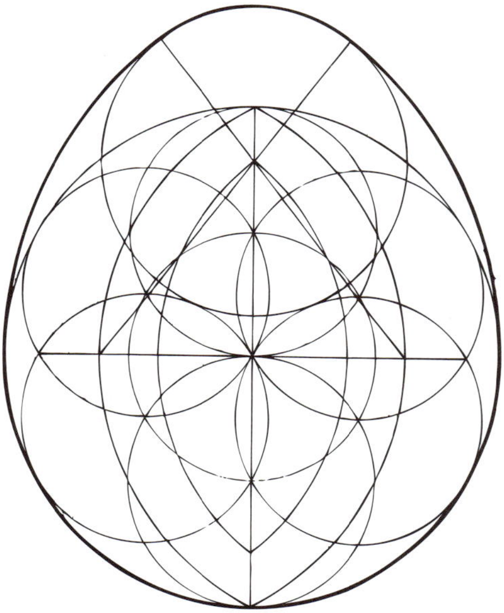

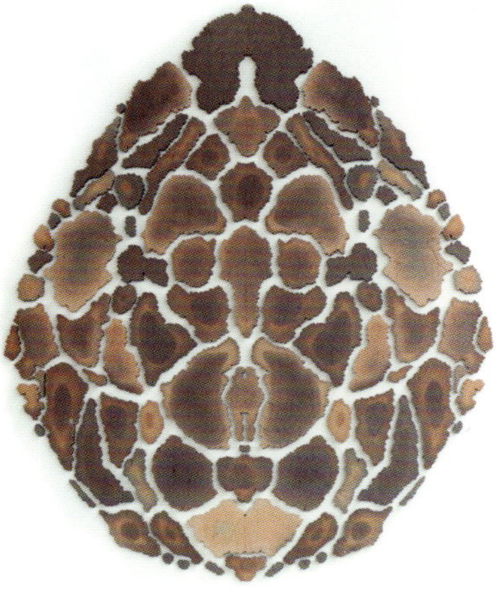

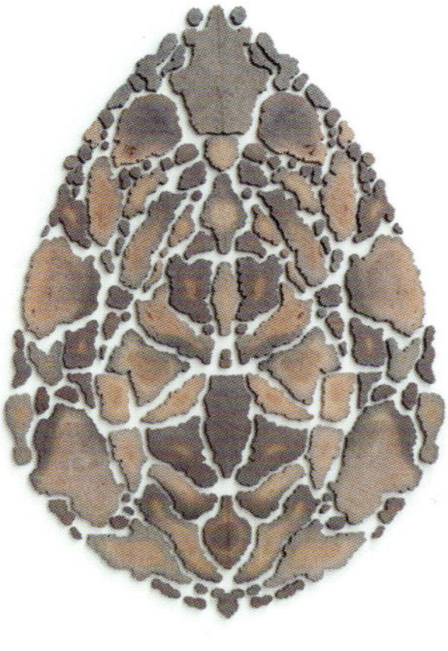

A geometric Golden Egg. Two of the Mind Map series. Photographs: Jonty Wilde.

Rocks in My Bed, 2005

Rocks in My Bed, named after the Duke Ellington song, brings together a range of ideas and influences. Randall-Page typically marks out boulders with paint prior to carving; this work extends that process, growing from his fascination with how the resulting designs appear on the stone surface. These particular lines are based on chemical reactions. Randall-Page likens their repeating but random patterns to improvisational jazz – taking a theme or motif and developing it away from the original concept whilst retaining a relationship with it. This also calls to mind the artist Paul Klee's notion of drawing being akin to 'taking a line for a walk'.

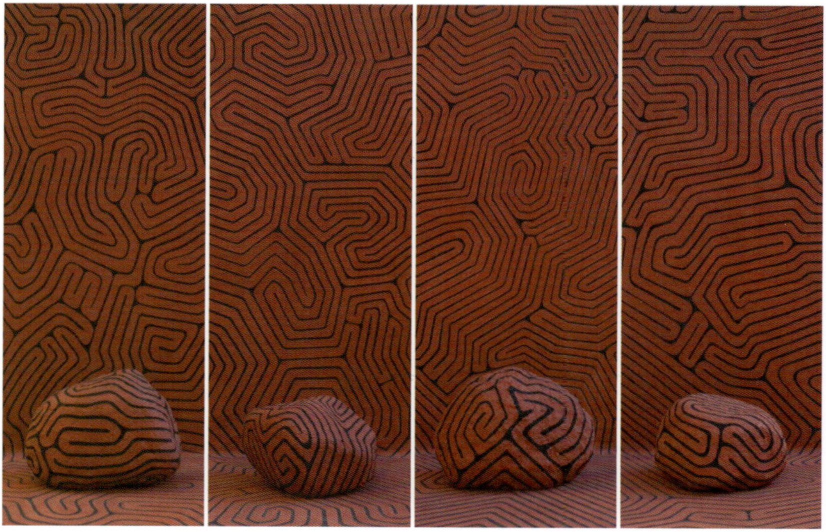

Rocks in My Bed, 2005. Photograph: Sally-Ann Norman.

Terminal Bud, 2009

Another series of incredible and complex growth patterns is revealed in the four charcoal drawings Terminal Bud. This term refers to any bud positioned at the tip of a plant stem. The cabbage is a particularly large terminal bud and allows us to see on a larger scale the intricacies of embryonic new growth found in all buds. Randall-Page frequently references his fascination with seeds and fruit; their potential and capacity as "containers of life in dormant form".[4] In these works this life is shown in development using a cross-section of a compact cabbage head. Magnified and made monotone, the familiar winding lines become abstract; we are forced to look anew and celebrate the extraordinary magnificence of this commonplace object.

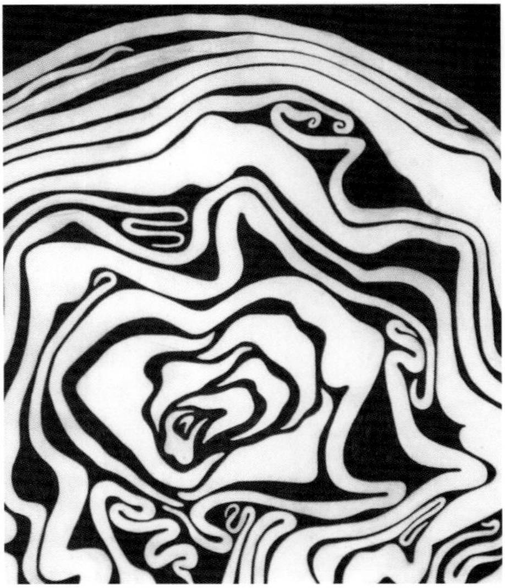

4 Peter Randall-Page in Conversation with Tessa Jackson. Yorkshire Sculpture Park 1992. pg 6

Terminal Bud (detail), 2009. Photograph: Dick Ellis.

Theme and Variation, 2008

This sequence of three works in bronze takes the idea of juxtaposing order and randomness in a new direction. Chaos is once again represented by glacial boulders but here the stones' presence is implied rather than actual. Randall-Page made fibreglass casts of boulders, introducing man-made uniformity by the application of thousands of ping pong balls to this skin, arranged in as regular a pattern as the depressions and rises in the stone allowed. A matt white finish lends stunning tonal range, with shadow and highlight created across the surface, both by these contours and by the endless sweep of the nodules. The works have the quality of simple, primordial beings, removed from the ruggedness of stone and made less tangible.

Music is again referenced in the title. The concept of theme and variation – the building of a cumulative visual vocabulary in this case – is pivotal to Randall-Page. He also likens the patterns on the surface of the works to jazz in the way the dots becomes lines, the lines become phrases and the sculpture is animated by this interplay of rhythm and movement.

Memory of Rain, 2006

Memory of Rain works on a very basic human level. It evokes a universal experience: seeing raindrops fall onto a puddle, lake or river, the still surface punctuated and animated by innumerable droplets. Without recourse to words this elaborate construction of thousands of small terracotta discs invites recognition and collective memory. Much of Randall-Page's work exists on a similar level, communicating physical ideas or metaphors, exploring the timeless things that make us human.

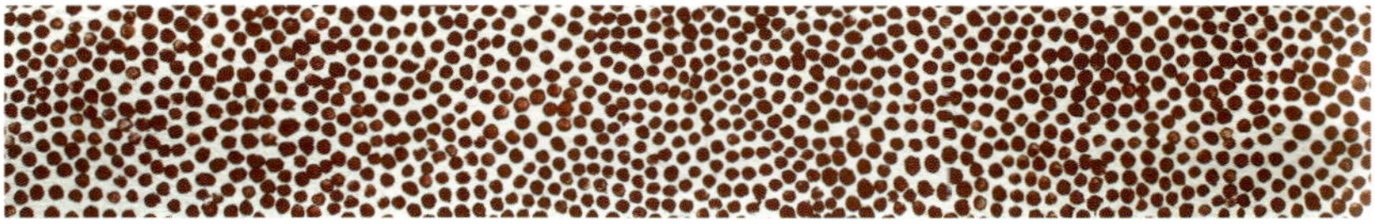

Memory of Rain, (detail of drawing) 2006. Photograph: Peter Randall-Page.

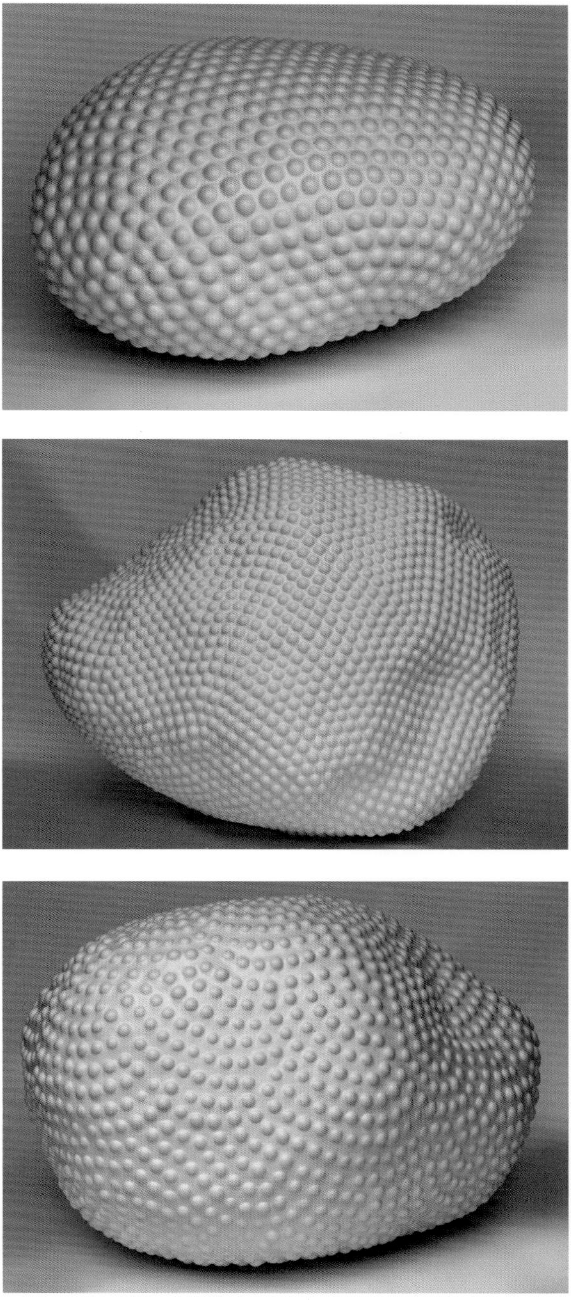

Theme and Variation I, II, III, 2008. Photographs: Steve Russell.

Open Air
In Mind of Monk, 2008

"The pattern carved into the surface of the three marble spheres corresponds to a system that has fascinated me and preoccupied my work for several years. I first came across it in scientific images at high magnification of liquids that won't mix. When put under pressure these liquids form beautiful patterns with distinct rules, one liquid forming a continuous line like the 'path' of a labyrinth, the other, like the 'hedge' can terminate or meet in junctions of three...

"As well as covering the entire surface of the spheres with lines of equal thickness without leaving any gaps, an additional self-imposed rule is that the labyrinth path is one continuous line rather than a series of interconnecting systems; you can follow it with your finger and get to the place you started.

"Interestingly the phenomena of the liquids not mixing is utilised by the organic world as the basis of all stripy patterns we see in nature. The stripes on a tigers and zebras, birds and fish, all originate from this chemistry. The pattern on the back of a mackerel is particularly faithful to the basic pattern...

"The zigzag pattern which gives the illusion of a faceted surface from a distance put me in mind of one of my favourite jazz musicians – Thelonious Monk – hence the title In Mind of Monk."[5]

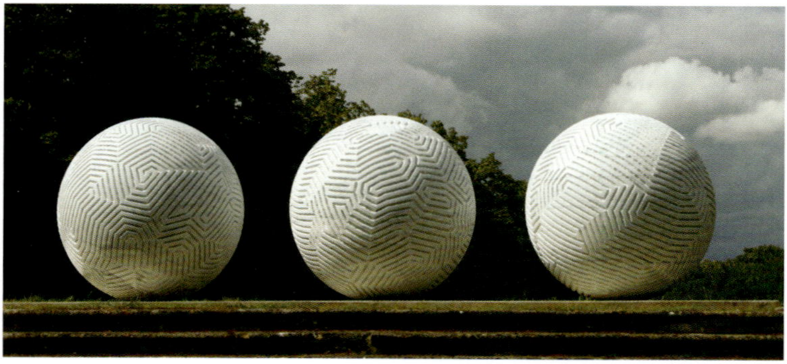

5 Artist's statement, July 2008.

In Mind of Monk, 2008. Loan: private collection, UK; courtesy Eleven Fine Art, London. Photograph: Peter Randall-Page.

Multiplication By Division, 2000

This work was one of the first to deal explicitly with the underlying structures affecting growth. It was described by Randall-Page as "a seminal piece for me and represents a new direction in my work concerning the geometry which underlies organic form."[6]

Like Shapes in the Clouds this work deals with Platonic solids – shapes which are rudimentary to the structure of the universe itself. Randall-Page has a keen interest in, "the relationship between singularity and multiplicity; how something can change from being one to being many".[7] As in cell division, this means each successive shape is a sub-division of the one before it, becoming increasingly more complex. These particular forms are described by the artist as nature's favourites which, "can be found in atomic and molecular structures as well as crystalline and cellular growth because they pack things together with optimum efficiency".[8]

The beautiful, soft, golden Cotswold stone used to make this work is called Guiting limestone.

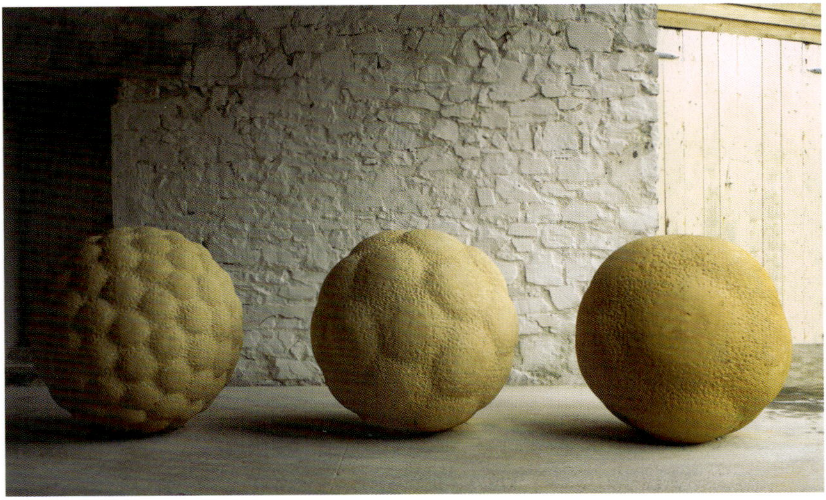

6 Artist's statement, May 2002. 7, 8 Ibid.

Multiplication By Division, 2000. Loan: courtesy Roger and Lyvie De Haan. Photograph: Peter Randall-Page.

Flayed Stone II and III, 1998

The *Flayed Stone* series employs glaciated granite boulders in a different way to the stones in gallery two. Rather than cutting lines into the surface to impose structure on it, these works have more sense of the interior. With coils as opposed to linear incisions, the stone appears softer, more sensual and of the body. As Randall-Page describes, they appear "like stones flayed to reveal sheets of muscle and sinew, they suggest the containment of pressure from beneath".[9] The great forces required to form the stone are echoed in the implied strength of these incredibly dense works.

By Another Ocean I, II, and III, 1998

This group of works relates to the large new sculpture *Corpus*, also in Kilkenny limestone. Thematically, the concern is with the endless line or loop, which has the potential to unravel at any time and therefore feels to be in a constant state of tension, pushing against an unseen skin that contains and confines it. The sculptures bear formal relationships with pupae or the abdomen of an insect.

Parting Company II and III, 1996

Made on his return from a three month visit to Australia during which he intensively studied botanical form, *Parting Company* are sculptures based on the way Eucalyptus seeds "break apart with exquisite precision to reveal their internal structure"[10]. Formally much closer to Randall-Page's earlier, more representational work, *Parting Company* are the result of a very specific experience and are the three-dimensional expression of a period of study when he did not make any sculpture. The stone is a type of hard golden limestone sourced from Pakistan.

9 Peter Randall-Page: New Sculpture and Drawings. Stephen Lacey Gallery 1998, pg 4.
10 Artist's statement March 2008

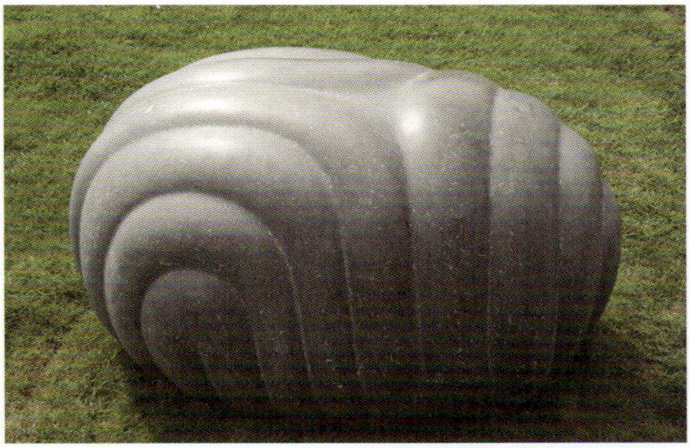

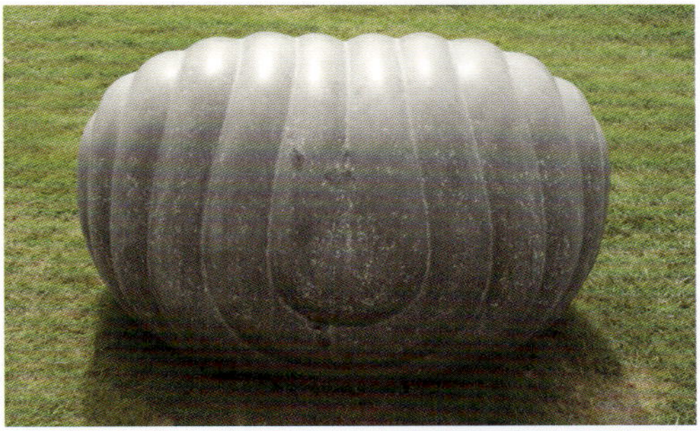

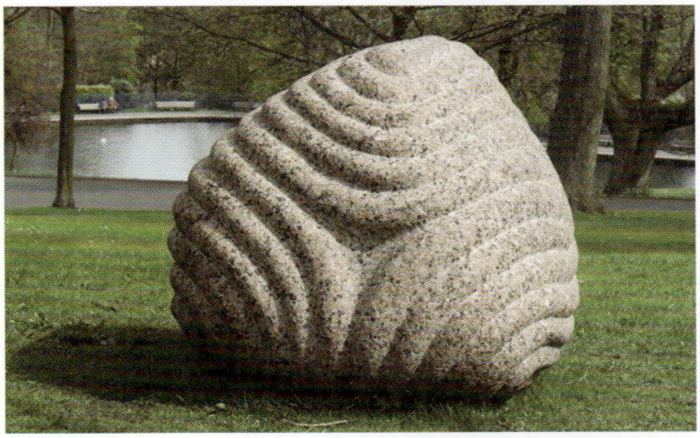

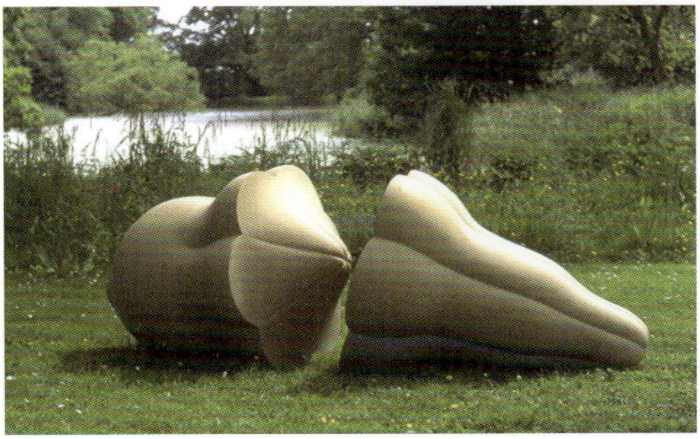

By Another Ocean II, 1998. By Another Ocean III, 1998. Flayed Stone II, 1998. Parting Company II, 1996.
Loan of By Another Ocean I, courtesy private collector. Photographs: Peter Randall-Page.

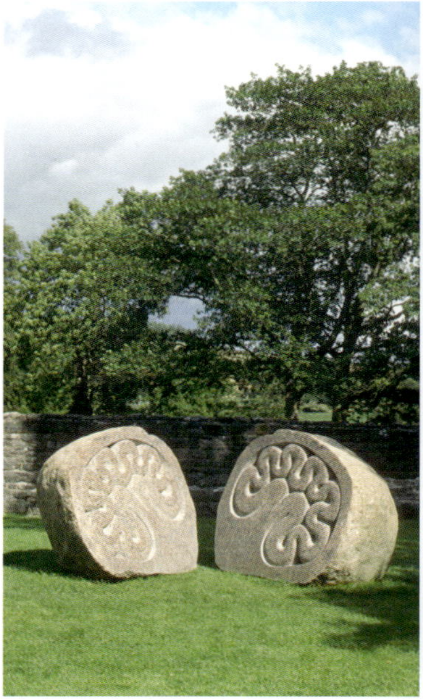

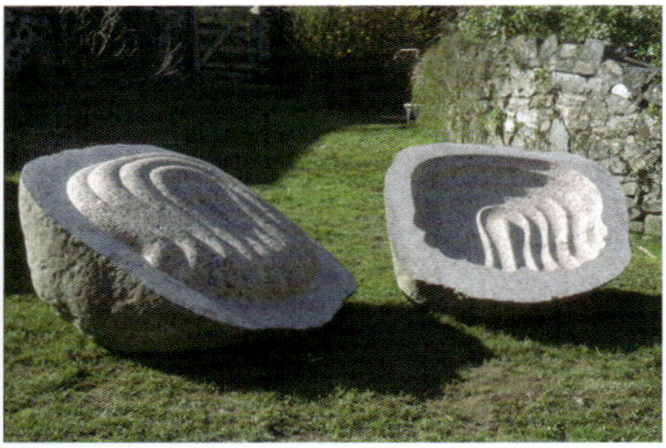

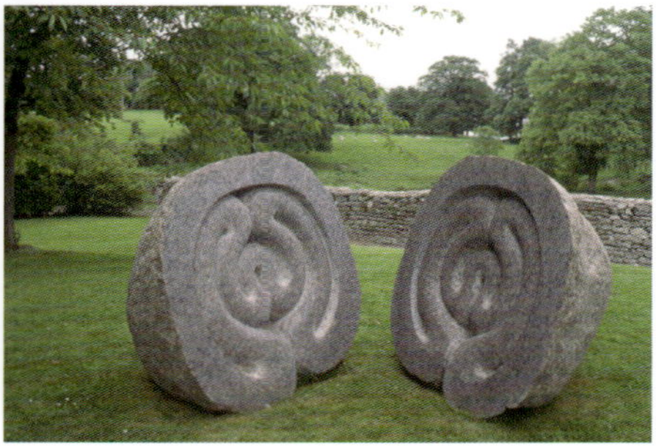

Clockwise from left: *Secret Life I*, *Secret Life VI*, *Secret Life III*. Photographs: Peter Randall-Page.

Secret Life IV, 1994

Part of a series of works made in the mid-1990s, Secret Life IV is an extension and development of Randall-Page's original concept of the carved split boulder. Here, the exploration of the inner surface encompasses both incised lines on the flat plane and much deeper carving into the body of the stone to create a palpable sense of it being an opened shell or the cleft body of a fruit, split to unveil its seed.

Secret Life IV reveals a series of bulbous nodules within its core and anticipates Randall-Page's later works that use repeated shapes and rhythmic regularity. Relationships to the body are also at the fore, the bulging spheres resembling the contoured lining of the intestines.

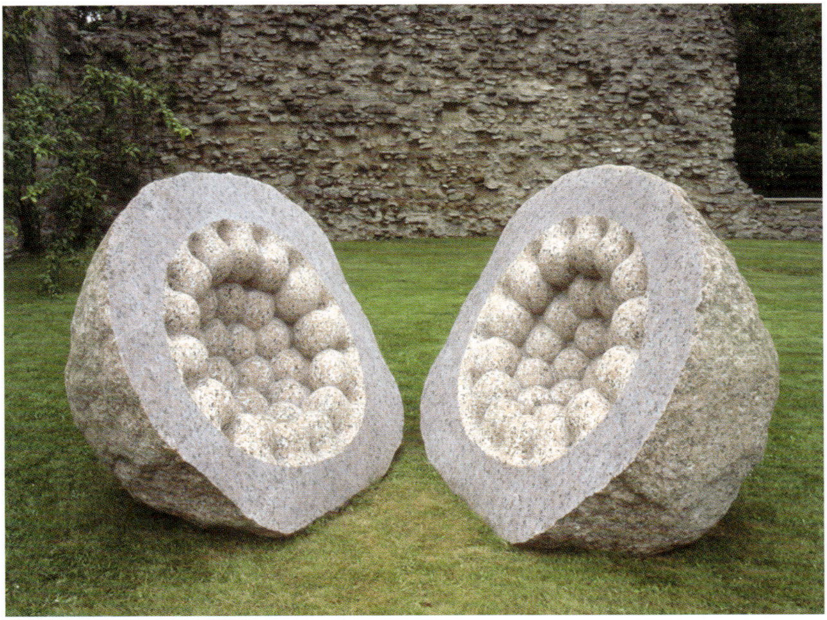

Secret Life IV, 1994. Loan courtesy Julian Francis. Photograph: Peter Randall-Page.

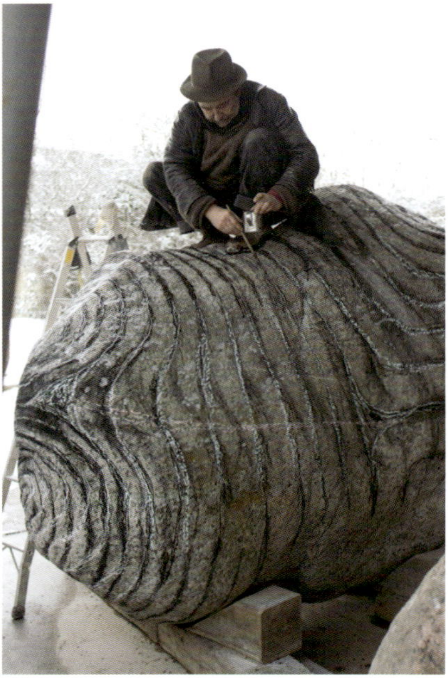

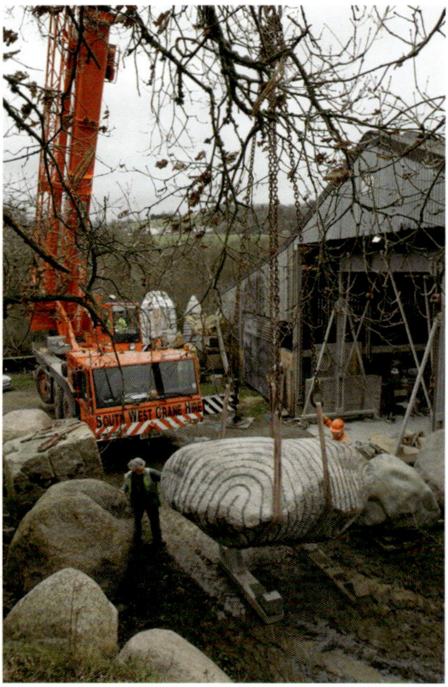

Peter Randall-Page working on Stone Dreaming, 2009.
Stone Dreaming being lifted by a crane at Peter Randall-Page's studio. Photographs: Chris Chapman.

Bronze Dreaming Stone, 2000
Stone Dreaming, 2009

These two works have a close and fascinating relationship with one another. Before it was carved to become Stone Dreaming the huge boulder was used in the creation of Bronze Dreaming Stone. Lengths of rope covered in molten wax were draped over its surface and a cast made of the resultant form; with the boulder removed a husk remained, like a spent carapace or the abandoned shell of a sea creature. The hollowness brings into play ideas of presence and absence, and the implied memory of form. When working in bronze, Randall-Page is always concerned about the material's tendency to suggest hollowness, but in this work the interior is opened up and the emptiness of the form made explicit.

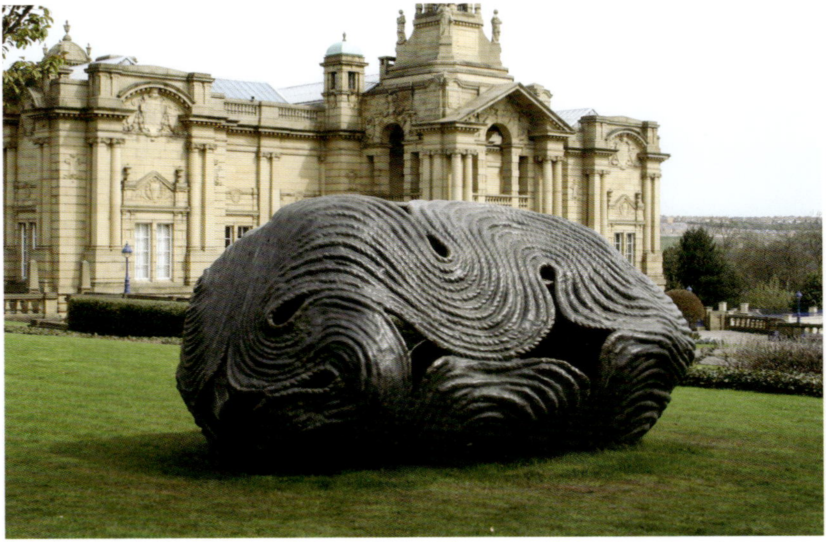

Bronze Dreaming Stone, 2000. Photograph: Peter Randall-Page.

Underground Gallery Project Space

"...by making little objects out of wax, plasticine or clay, I test things out, discarding ideas that I am not so interested in and concentrating my effort on forms that seem to have the most potential."[11]

Peter Randall-Page has never before shown the range of models, maquettes and sketchbooks assembled here. They reflect his creative process and the development of shapes and ideas, the endless honing of expressive possibilities. Many of the models for works in the YSP exhibition are displayed, including Mother Tongue, Fructus and Corpus, and several reveal practical concerns, having pins and calculations for scaling up to the full sized versions. Other pieces simply reveal areas of interest to the artist – the tiny figurative sculptures evoke associations with ancient artifacts and iconic works such as the ancient carving, the Willendorf Venus. The small, spherical clay pots abound with a sense of joy in material; each bears the marks of the artist's fingers where it was held before his thumb was plunged into the soft clay. However simple, these objects explore significant themes – positive and negative space, and the exposed interior.

Clay Body, 2009, is a new series of work in which Randall-Page has taken thrown clay cylinders and collapsed them using both hands simultaneously in a mirrored and almost unconscious action. The resulting sculptures have a slightly skewed symmetry as they fall in sensuous, fleshy folds. Repeated over and over again, this process has a real immediacy and, unlike carving, is quick to complete.

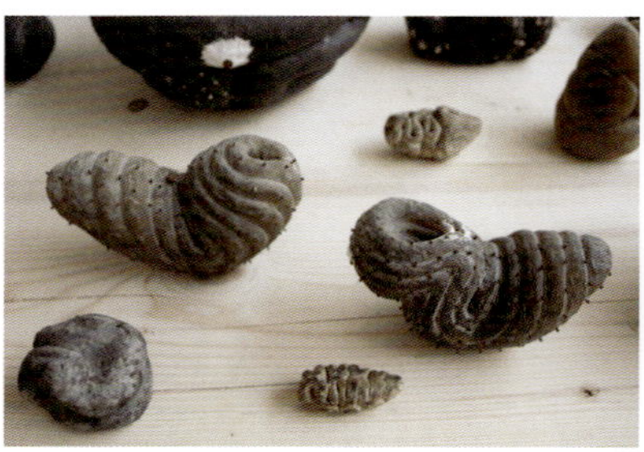

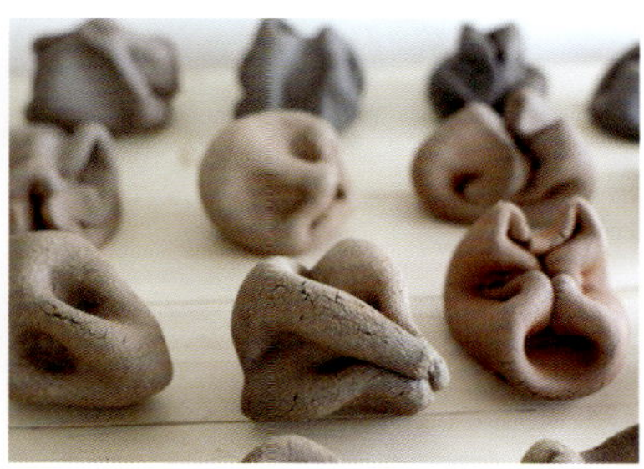

11 Peter Randall-Page in Conversation with Tessa Jackson. Yorkshire Sculpture Park 1992. pg 7.

Maquettes and models. Pieces from the Clay Body series. Photographs: Jonty Wilde.

Garden Gallery

The Garden Gallery features a selection of prints, drawings and small scale sculptures which support the main display, revealing different treatments and expressions of major themes from the coil and husks to Euclidian geometry and insect forms. Smaller in scale, Randall-Page's prints are incredibly accomplished and he moves with ease from very immediate, bold linocuts to the delicacy and lightness of touch required in etchings such as A Place of One's Own, 1994.

Also on display in this gallery are working drawings and models for the artist's Seed sculpture made for the Eden Project. In 2003 Randall-Page was appointed to work alongside Jolyon Brewis from Grimshaw Architects to develop a new education building; the brief was to create a building that was like a tree, illustrating the inspiration that can be drawn from botanical form. Randall-Page's keen appreciation of the fundamental mathematical principles that determine growth meant he was able to bring these concepts to the development of a roof structure which utilises the Fibonacci sequence, the golden proportion and their relationship to spiral phyllotaxis – the particular pattern of growth seen on the heads of sunflowers amongst many other things. Botanical imagery was introduced in a manner that went beyond the superficial and was pivotal in making the roof structure viable.

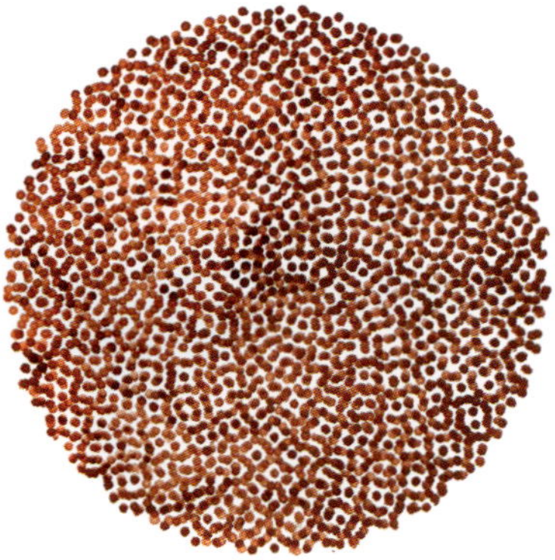

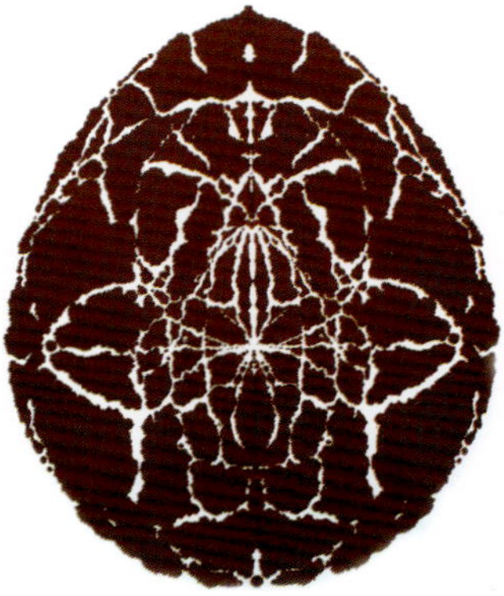

Fibonacci Flip, 2003. Euclidian Egg VI, 2008. Photographs: Peter Randall-Page.

1954 Born, Essex

1973-77 Studied at Bath Academy of Art

1977 Begins a correspondence with Isamu Noguchi

1977-78 Worked with Barry Flanagan; moved to London

1979 Worked at Wells Cathedral on conservation of 13th century sculpture

1980 Won Travelling Fellowship to the marble quarries of Carrara

1981 Participates in Objects and Sculpture at Arnolfini and the ICA with Edward Allington, Richard Deacon, Antony Gormley, Anish Kapoor and Bill Woodrow.

1982-8 Visiting Lecturer at Brighton Polytechnic

1982 First public commission for Leicester Royal Infirmary

1984 Participates in Attitudes '84 at Yorkshire Sculpture Park

1985-86 New Milestones project with Common Ground

1986 Three Fruit, first large Kilkenny limestone work

1987 Moves to Devon

1989-96 Local Distinctiveness project, Common Ground

1991 Series of important works in Kilkeny limestone, including New Touchstone and Where the Bee Sucks

1992 Sculpture and Drawings 1980-1992, Leeds City Art Gallery and YSP

1993 Visiting Lecturer at Royal College of Art, London
Where the Bee Sucks acquired by Tate

1994 Artist in residence, Tasmanian School of Art, University of Tasmania

1995 Three works on paper purchased by Tate

1999 Awarded Honorary Doctorate of Arts, University of Plymouth

2000 Inner Compulsion, significant sculpture for Millennium Seed Bank

2001 Turf maze at Burghley Sculpture Garden, Lincolnshire

2002-05 Associate Research Fellow, Dartington College of Arts

2003-05 Member of the design team for The Core education building, Eden Project

2004 Sung-Woon, commission for the Gwangju Biennale, Korea

2006 Give and Take wins Marsh Award for public sculpture, selected by the PMSA.
Mind's Eye, commission for Cardiff University Department of Psychology – first piece using fired clay tiles in a wall work

2007 Ruwenzori Sculpture Foundation Residency on Lolui Island, Uganda.
Seed, seventy tonne sculpture installed at the Eden Project

ACKNOWLEDGEMENTS

The efforts and generosity of many people have made this exhibition possible. Most importantly I want to thank Peter Murray and Clare Lilley for inviting me to exhibit my work in and around the magnificent Underground Gallery, and Sarah Coulson who, with the curatorial team at YSP, has worked so hard on the show and this publication.

Special thanks are due to all the individuals and organisations that have agreed to loan work and given financial support to the exhibition.

The technical team at YSP under Alan Mackenzie and Iain Stephenson have been a real pleasure to work with; endlessly patient and highly professional together with energetic and enthusiastic volunteers.

My deepest gratitude must go to my own amazing team, Jennifer Mullins and Jane Hocking who have masterminded everything from my office; PJ Dove, David Brampton-Greene and Ben Adams who have worked above and beyond the call of duty to produce the work over an extended period of intensive effort.

Also, special thanks are due to Simon Thomas, Noel Wheadon, Reece Ingram, Hatt Reiss and Paul Devon Young for their wonderful help with the final stages.

Last but by no means least, I want to thank my lovely wife Charlotte for her endless support and encouragement and for putting up with me.

Peter Randall-Page, June 2009

PETER RANDALL-PAGE AT YORKSHIRE SCULPTURE PARK, SUPPORTED BY:

Romulus Construction Ltd // The Henry Moore Foundation
Friends of Yorkshire Sculpture Park // Simon & Virginia Robertson
The Roger De Haan Charitable Trust // Julian Francis
Gay McGuinness // Edward Miller and Monina von Opel

Published to coincide with

PETER RANDALL-PAGE

AT YORKSHIRE SCULPTURE PARK

27 JUNE 2009 – JANUARY 2010
UNDERGROUND GALLERY & LAWN / GARDEN GALLERY

ISBN 978-1-871480-75-7

Text: Clare Lilley, Sarah Coulson
Book design & production: Sarah Coulson
Editing: Peter Randall-Page, Clare Lilley
Proofing: Angie de Courcy Bower, Adrianne Neil, Helen Pheby, Alma Zevi
Print: Derek Hattersley & Son, Hoylandswaine, UK

www.ysp.co.uk
www.peterrandall-page.com

Yorkshire Sculpture Park
West Bretton, Wakefield, West Yorkshire, WF4 4LG

Yorkshire Sculpture Park receives funding from Arts Council England, Wakefield Metropolitan District Council, and West Yorkshire Grants (a joint committee of Bradford, Calderdale, Kirklees, Leeds and Wakefield Councils). YSP is an Accredited Museum and Registered Charity, number 1067908.